# Allelopathy

By Kevin Gorman

"Go then, there are other worlds than these."
- Stephen King, *The Gunslinger*

# Acknowledgements

Like so many wonderful and horrifying things, Allelopathy came fairly well out of nowhere. I suppose we'll let you decided which category it ultimately rests under.

This book wouldn't have been possible without my longtime friend and editor, Heidi Elaine Kirby. I don't know what I would do without you—in either aspect.

A special bit of thanks is reserved for Amy Kathryn Baker, Heidi's sister, who lent her skills for the cover of this book. It's nice to have someone capable at the helm.

In that same vein, so much of my life is result of my amazing family—with a special welcome to my two new sisters, Jaclyn and Lindsay. I love you all very much. Your support has really kept me in the fight.

That's what it's about, though, in the end—those people who love you enough to drag you until you're able to walk.

I'd also like to thank Lauren D'Oliveira, Team Funishment, The Schwartz, the boys, Kenny Gallow, and anyone beautiful enough to express themselves without fear.

Eternally,

Kevin Gorman
Sandusky, Ohio, January 2016

# Table of Contents

## I.

I'LL TELL YOU AS A GIVEN THAT YOU LOVE THE
WAY I'M LIVING.
MY LOVE CAN SHATTER WORLDS, SLAY CANCER,
AND CURE THE BLUES —
FORGIVES THE UNFORGIVEN.

SORRY, I'M CONFUSED —
I THINK IT'S THE KILL
DESCRIBING ITSELF SO WELL.
RISING ON THE SMOKE OF THE HEALED.

# Alazaki

Chewing plastic,
sighing as it cuts the gum.
It's all that could be done.

A fondness for the creep
colored confused.
Taken and subdued.

With a disposition for
the things that made
no sense.

Seductive laughter
reverberating through
the great hall of small things.

A whispered dream,
slithered wet, over teeth
that dared to bite.

# If You Show Me Yours

Sometimes, she wore crystals charged
with a thousand empty promises.
They were more for show than glow.
She felt less afraid with them on,
like sunglasses or a hat pulled low
to cover the fact that they know...

Don't they?

She came around when he got lonely,
but he never got lonely enough.
She ached for meaning
the way his tooth ached from eating
all that sugary nonsense—

Man, FUCK diabetes.

He was ugly on the outside;
she was lovely on the inside.

So, they made it work.

She needed a connection,
and they'd never make much sense of it,
but sense is for the banal and unfulfilled.

In the mirror,
he saw the reason there was no She.
She saw it, too,
but it was an arrangement that was fluid,
like vapor on the breeze.

The doctor said he had a heart murmur,
but she thought it was more of a seductive whisper.
She romanticized the broken,
and he understood this vaguely,
but he never tried to fix her.

"Nothing is sexier than sad,"
he'd mumble, unrepentant.

He was coffee trying to explain itself to tea.

He liked his coffee the way she liked her men,
but they'd pretend.

Sometimes, when the night grew long,
like he never did,
She'd remember what it was like to be wanted,
undaunted, and speckled with choices.

Sometimes, he'd remember to forget,
and then sleep a couple of hours.
Of course, the nights were short,
the way their love always was...

The winner got to pick dinner.

It helped maintain the cause.

# Intervention

I was no longer humble in the eyes of God.
It was a precarious situation,
drawn out and ripe.

It wouldn't be sweet,
but it would surely be juicy.

He had plenty of proof...
Of course, so did that whiskey.
The bourbon tasted of lies, too,
in case you were wondering...

Mind wandering...

Mine your mind, Child.
Sound advice.

# On Punctuality

The Clock only really functioned when it felt like it,
and the damned thing reeked of arrogance and knowing.
It knew far more than I ever cared to tell it.

There were demons in there.
The bitter sadness of fighting and losing
again
and again
and again

Self aware.

The Clock would often be accused of being far too self
aware.

Guilty.

It was a given that, on nights like this,
they'd drive to Lookout Point.
You can see for miles...

They'd number the stars...

Of course, the Clock, being forgetful
and teeming with unexpressed self-loathing,
would make them late to the party.

Sometimes, the Clock's watch would get lippy,
and they needed to be separated.
It caused quite a scene,
and no one likes a scene,
except for the Clock.

Every now and again,
the Clock got very drunk and beat his inner child.
The neighbors don't even bother
calling 911 anymore.
There was no such thing as help,
unless you were the Clock.
Help was like bacon and eggs.

The Clock was never late to breakfast.

# Knowing

Heaved the burden from his chest and wiped the sweat
from his brow,
"I'll bleed for the rest if they answer my call."
Sunken shrieks of shores grown dim.
He bathed in the moment while her worry wore thin.
It's time to hurry nightscapes of the wonder within.


Make her believe...


He knew the fear long, and the doubt wagered well.
"Start fresh and begin," like you never even fell.
He said, "You know, I don't know, but I do have a
guess..."
She knew the song well, but he knew it the best.
Fall uphill for the thrill of scaling,
"I am love, and I am hope,"
came the word softly spoken.

In his mind, he held her like tomorrow never mattered.
Laughter, shrugs shrill...

For now and thereafter.

# Frequently Seeking

There was still love in spite of the complications.
The prognosis was psychosis,
so he went back to faking.
"Fake it 'til you make it,"
sharpen the blade, aching.

There were spirits calling numbers
that were already punched.
Lurched agony on the water,
never went under once.
Looking like a cigarette taken
straight to the lungs.

Happiness comes...

Release the trigger for reality
or maybe a touch.
In any case, the end was open,
and it felt like her trust—

Fleeting over the years
and increasing each month.


Believers slanted sickly—
"They rebuild you above..."


So he hoped,
fingers and limbs twisted and broke.
They took the word of the monster,
but the monster was drunk.

## II.

i JUST WANTED TO HELP YOU BECAUSE
i'VE SEEN YOUR FACE BEFORE.
iN THE MiRROR.

THERE ARE OTHERS, TOO...

BUT, RiGHT NOW, YOU ARE
THE ONLY ONE WHO MAKES SENSE
THE PROBLEM WRUNG AND RiNSED.

i TRiED TO TAKE iT FROM YOU
AND GiVE YOU HOPE.

# Flexing

I defected from the demons,
glaring angry with disgust,
claws at the door.
From others
not the same,
but nonetheless...

So close now.
Always so close.
Sometimes it gets to me,
and I have to back away.
I had to get angry—
Then, we lost the other shore yesterday.

I'm not sure what it means,
but it won't be long now...

No one cares about secrets anymore.
Francis told me that he loved me today.

He didn't mean it.
I wish he would have.


When there was still love in the world,
I would have wanted it
to hold a different meaning.

# This poem is called Whitley Strieber is an Asshole

A man famous for his alien abduction experiences,
once told me that I was crazy.


I think it was him, anyway.
I suppose it could have been a pod person
or the ghost of one.
I'm not really sure.


I am certain, though, that he recommended I see a specialist.
There were two of them.
I wasn't really sure who to trust.


I asked them something only Jesus would know.
They washed my feet and were very gentle and kind.
It made me feel important.


It was a magical summer.

# Bad Kitty

That's a poor little kitty
if I ever did see one.
His whiskers are splintered and twisted.
He loped along like he was too big for his body.

Sometimes, the human came and offered
food not fought for.
It pleased him to feel full.

His paws held claws so sharp—
he could end it.
His human had no idea
what he had seen.

Instead, she put out another bowl of water.

Some days, she gave him reason to believe.
Silly, Kitty doesn't understand the world.
Nothing is free.

He would hurt for his water —
though it never drowned his hope.


Kitties are silly, I thought I told you.
She called him "Patches,"
never realizing how fitting it was.


When the human left,
There was an empty ration left behind—
bought and sold for tails that flick and wind.

# Creature from the Ether

Dreams shuffled forth in awkward waves.
They were as real as you or me.
Fuck, they were twice as real as my friend, Carrot,
but I didn't hold that against him.

The universe is fickle and apathetic.
Pure strangeness at work is beyond
human capacity to imagine.

One of the earliest notions to keep you worried and
awake,
seemed to be the very real situation involving
the ether and the mischief.
These merrymaking mesmers,
cutting humor of the random.

Startling to think about.

After all, if the universe refuses
to take itself seriously, well. . .

I'm afraid it's
"Fuck 'em and feed 'em fruitloops" time...

Creeping Jesus.  I found a friend.
He's a little real and a bit pretend.

He makes me feel like it all might work out,
if we believe.

Of course,  if it all works out;
the movie they make about it
will be a bit boring.

No one likes a boring movie,
unless Elijah Wood is in it.
He'd probably cry a lot and walk around.
Nerds the world over would worship him
as their messiah.

Because sometimes, boring books
become boring movies.
But,  it helps to pass the time.

# MIB

There were midgets in the Earth in those days...
Men on the mend.
Radiant shards wept from the eyes of stars,
and the lights danced on the breeze.

The sway of tree and sense of ease,
long since reserved for the unaware...
until they're here...

The rancid and repugnant shuffle forward
from shadows in the night.

Oh, and the walk-ins,
how wretchedly droll.

There's light, too.
It threatens to burst from
the hearts of men
and many who aren't men at all.

There has got to be some semblance
of unity here.

The field has conformed.
Bet the field, forlorn.

The King is dead.
Seduced by Siren's breath,
throaty and heaved against rock.
Vessels long since lost to rot.

Still, the lights danced on the breeze.

There were Nazis in South America
in those days.
Ahhhh, the dog days of Günter.
Bells tolled toward the moon.

And what of that?

It seemed every bit as real as the sweet caress of steel,
finger-wrapped knuckle cracks of
hesitating love.

You can't go back.

When you love evil and it loves you
and there's no one above you. . .
You cough and wheeze and suck through
any instance of regret...

Do not forget...

There are strange men wearing large hats
that belie their arrogance.
They speak in thick accents,
but it's gibberish,  anyway.

They should not be trusted.

# Oh

I think he probably preferred climbing sideways
because it really went against the grain.

Flying flags. . .
not the false sort, though.
Real, hard-working American-made flags,
sporting cameras capturing me being free.

The key is not to move—
you see?

Their vision is based on movement
or something.
I don't really know.

Are you going to be long?

# Rain Man

This time was special—
needs wrapped lengthy
in deeds paid hungry
to free forces struggling to breathe,
dark and starless these streets.

CNN on the mend—
was still not naming his friend.
Lashed cross tangled tongue,
Fast,
held broken at last...
and the hour of knowing.

Soft targets and,  boy,  baby—
they were soft.
The pigs did well;
Finally, a reason to shell—
"Got 'em,  we'll make the news,"
lead spread wild and loose.

By the way...

We bombin'...

Left the trigger full of liquor
"Done," they called it.
The yuppies wet
would finally regret the steel slept.
Damages wept—
I left—
Now, forget I saw it.

All he learned,
wanted to say, but it burned.
Wasn't right on the night
the big hit the herd —
just when the death
hit the land,
plagued.

Shredded and worn by the sand;
here are the numbers,  my man,

"We're short."

Demons dreaming the war.
Terror loud on blast.
Broken somber and fast.

Wretched hunger empty.
Mixing the blood with the ash.

# RepLicants

It isn't plausible,
but it's possible.
It's in their faith to do these things.

Lies rise in a wave with the heat.
Strung along for retreat.
Bread crumbs leading
to places we'll never be.

The cattle taste like Kobe—
not the beef,
But my soul, B.
"He didn't do that shit!"
I know, G.
So, let 'em have his trophy.

They said he was on his way out.
He said the same thing.
They were right.

We all are—
but this isn't a game.

This is the real, yo,
where victims rise like
a crescendo.
It's midnight in the desert,
but it's going down in Africa.
I'd teach you all a lesson,
but I'm kind of scared of ya.

Now, let me change it up
and tell you a story like I knew you.
You see, the CIA will grow you—
terror-wrapped,
packed, and loaded.
Sell the story to the world,
while they straight up
fucking snow you.

"Come on, man—that's below you."

Let the bakers bake a luscious cake
of "You don't know me."

I know 'em, though.
You see, I've been around—
I've seen the towers fall and smolder
from the shoulders of disorder—
wrapped and relished,
made to order.

There's no monster under there,
but the bogeyman is here—
color ravaged by your fear.

Blood-flushed cheeks
so crystal clear.
Sustained and strengthened—
did I mention...
by the sword and with exemption
for the word's long held contention,
that if you don't talk about and mention—
their lives weren't really lost?

I found them.

You will find me
fear behind me
at the bell curve with Bill Hicks.
We'll be waiting,  contemplating,
while their lies destroy your kids.

## III.

SOUGHT ETERNAL,
A DECADE SHADED,
GRIMY MURAL
LEFT FOR THE FUTURE TO DETERMINE.
HE USED TO DREAM LIKE HE WAS CERTAIN.
NOW, HE DOESN'T SLEEP,
MOST OF THE TIME, HE'S HURTING.

# Diving

It was always dark in the room.
Light broke the peace, but it was quickly ushered
away.
There was cancer in the barrel
loaded up with malaise.

And shots rang out...

A flash in the darkness—
It's coming...

Trapped again in the room
but gaining ground.
Flipping a switch called "Survival,"
Running...
Running...

Never knowing who was chasing
or running away.

Always knowing it was ugly,
so ugly...

Shots rang out...

A chorus from the end
exploded within,
wrapped to diffuse the echo,
Recoil, my friend.
So sharp now that it's lost...
forever damned.
Played out weekly—
Drifting—
In.
Out.
In...

# Autumn

Sunken face,  splintered red
like the lines of his gaze.
In haste,
tried to remember his fate...
drawn and left at the brink of the gate.

Nobody waits—
when the dawn drips,
wallowing,  speckled white lips—
glance from her to her hip.

Jagged was the blade
that bled the man—
under the depths of dismay—
become her...

Drunk on the taste,
dismissing the shakes.

Wishing
my life you would take.
Kissing—
I'd risk it all over again.
The bliss—
beginning of end.


I said, "She'd destroy me."
You said, "She already did."

# Wolves

Go for the throat—
teeth out—
I wrote you a note.
Crazy, loaded, and locked in the shell—
Bled hungry and empty as Hell—
It burns just the same...

Fractured memories of her and the days,
shrugged, with a smile lacking faith.
Love is above and below you the same.

Tears choked, wretched—
the taste—
empty my eyes out again.

I need to hate you,
and I never will.
I must replace you with something
Other than pills.

Sometimes, I still
taste you fresh upon my lips.
These times I need and want to hate you,
but I chase you again.

Running low on the blood in this pen,
drained, but so full of it.
Strained forever again.
There are pieces of you on the wind;
anything to make the memory end.

You can layer your pity on bread,
spread it,
and layer it again.
Eat that shit knowing
you'll choke on the time you said, "Friend."

See, I was zoning—
bought and sold me—
smoke to the dome
and barely smoldering.

I'd curse the fire went out,
well aware it's my only.

In the end,
I won't do a fucking thing.
I need you to be
the thing that I just can't believe.
Grunting, I roll up my sleeves,
push on like I'm riding the breeze...

I died the day I lost the lie.

# Trapped

Worry was a favorite.
So much of it, sometimes.
Once, the Worry stayed far too long.
It shuffled forward from the shadows,
blood- drenched and shivering.

Rummaging about in the darkness
leaves one open to bloody knees.

I' m flying on the back of
a wind called *discontent*.

# Lamb of Sod

Sacrifice on the altar
of the memory of her touch.
It happens way too much.

Just yesterday, I choked the life from
a dream dripped raw.
I slashed its throat and let the love
drain slow.

What's your name?

Forgive me,  I think I know,
you're from a place inside my soul.
Two Thursdays ago,  you sat
corner- cat,
just three tables from my own.
It feels like home.

I love you as I breathe,
but when you turned to leave,

I crossed my fingers—
still, it lingers...


Fresh upon my mind's eye,
and steady like your gaze.
The war was waged.
Turn the page.


You see now,
I was choking
on the irony softly spoken.
Though, I function,
I'm still broken.


The truth will find you,
and you will suffocate
beneath its force.


He's a joke to all who know him,
and you showed him,
oh,
you showed him.

Bright, the memory tinged golden.

Then one day, everything changed.

I lost you in the storm.
The fog slipped slowly
upon the shores of never will—
I've had my fill.

You will, too—
there was only you.
But, now there's me—
Don't you see?

Don't pretend you don't.
Don't pretend—I know!
Consumed while entombed—
dust, alone.

# Mirrors

He was simple in his ways,
fingers outstretched,  ever-reaching.
No one was ever reaching back.

He bit his lip and whispered my name...

I feed.

He was what they wanted him to be;
I mainlined his hope and shot
a hot spike I never wanted.

I took him
and showed him promise.
It felt good,
just not for him.

Some days,  I get sad
when I remember.

Most days, I try to forget—
I took the world from him.

I need you to know I wish it would work.
I tried so hard to make it right...
but the truth is, he is useless—

aside from laughs and cheers
Quaked and shaken.
Rumbled down to the ground.
Setup a compound
on the brink of Mistaken.

So, I pretended...

I showed him all he could be,
took it away just as quickly,
reminded him of his place.

I'll never love you.

Probably, no one will.

I was the spark struck in darkness,
illuminating everything that
will never be.
So, I breathe.


That breath felt good,
chased the memory away.

# Wormen

Struggling, he shrugged
shards hanging clear.

They were back.
They always came back.

Half a nap or so,
maybe a lifetime ago,
glistening steel smoked
and gagged at the throat.
Rasp, choke.

Midnight on a brand new day—
what do you say?
Brought back again;
I feel them within.

A wheeze, regurgitated goo
squirming a frantic dart
toward the half- cried moon.

Splitting the rest,
summer waves rise and crest.

This city is fucking ugly,
and I deserve it.
Fingers, a firm-fit
glove of tongues
pulling at the tale.

Pepper-ground pasta
with all the benefits
but none of the tradition.

A boot came down.

Satisfying and defying—
calmly trying...
I'm not lying!

You'll find me in the land where
the sun sets gray.

Break the haze.

Death isn't pleasing,
except when it is.
The memory always came
about now.

I am eternal,
and I am damned.
See you, Auntie.

Oh, I'll see you again,
shriveled stench wet
on the wind.

I thought I saw you
yesterday in the rain.

It was just my inner child.

## IV.

RADIANT, I WAVED HER GAZE AWAY.
SHRUGGED TOMORROW OFF MY SHOULDERS
IN THE FACE OF TODAY.

WRETCHED AT LUNCH,
LOSING MY TOUCH,
SICK FROM THE PILLS,
AND KNOWING TOO MUCH.

SET ABLAZE WITH A TOUCH,
BROKEN AND DROWNING IN RUST.

# BetWeen

Dearest Emily,


I do not know from where I am reaching out right now.
They say if we write,
messages have a way of
trickling
down
to
where they need to go.


So, here you find me.


I don't have time to say much.
I'm up for patrol in five minutes.

# Presents

Everything is waiting now—
everything bears your touch.
I looked for you in my dreams last night...

If I don't find you,  I will follow
to other worlds than these.

And I wait...

Love,  it's not pleasant hoping
to find your heart again—
it's not comforting not knowing,
if we'll meet or it's pretend.

Some would say you ruined me—
I call these people honest.
Some would say,
"Twas Voodoo,"
that unleashed your force upon us.

I'm not alone...
Real love suffers with me...

A part of me that I used to love so,
so doggedly beneath the droning—
I drink the water in,
lift my chin,
and forget that I am drowning.

Some days,  the end is pleaded for and celebrated.
Other days,  I think I'll speed it up
and wait for you in the ether.
You probably don't think that's right —
And honestly? I don't either.

# Scarred in the Rain

There was really little reason for him to creep after the
climax.
A billion smiles saved for her or whomever.

A wink and a nod and a "no one is ever up to any fun."
Not when it's time to lie.

No delight in the role,
probably, deservedly so.
An irony stretched thin and ready
to burst with laughter beneath the load.

In his mind, he was downright adequate.

The scabs are good
up until and just beside the thought.
There really wasn't much bad these days.

The thought was sickly sweet,
the acrid vapor of doubt
settling softly upon the tongue.
**Who** wasn't really important.
It was vital, though.

The body cries out.
A lurch of littered dust
cried by eyes long since dried.
Weeping sulfur at every hour
of this night.

A fool once said that the night time
is the right time.
It's certainly chock full of grit,
served with eggs on lazy church days.

Pretending that they didn't do what they did,
so, they grin and they give...
'cause their god forgives...

Crocodile typhoons of epic rotation
slink slowly from the corners
of the lies they live.

That brain damaged invalid over there
can't seem to tell up from down.

This will have to do.

He walked toward the exit,
but he wasn't going anywhere.

# Ignorance

He thought about the underground,
carved on a heart of stone,
ground to a fade
and displaced.

When the clown died,
the Earth shook.
Radiated memories dusted white
while the kiddies in the sandbox
fought on well into the night.

That was all there was to know, though.
Knowing much beyond that
would prove counterproductive
and frail.

A smothered doll with
a southern drawl
Whispered dreams directly into the ear
of a man, deaf for years...

But, the vibration was sultry
and available.

# You got jokes?

The vapor twisted again,
trailed off to a place he had been.
A goner no longer—but sick.
Ball vicious, fuck the bitches,
half a dollar —
Gave him change so
he could live.
Spotted, alone on the edge—
and you can see him 'til this day.

He didn't know where here was,
but he'd always been there.
A howl as he bends words and worlds,
robbed of his worth.

A farmhouse ugly against the rise
and crumbled to earth—
He lived mostly inside.

One day, he started to see the man.
He would always see him,
gaunt, kicking dust up in the wind.
Oh no—I forgot you again.
What did you say you'd like to be called?

You tell me.
In truth, I'm appalled—
emptiness clenched in his jaw...

He swallowed it, but it would
not sustain him.

I called out a greeting as he crested the hill.
Went retreating, path back beating—
I knew that look too well.
No more bleeding,
left dry when he fell.

When his back was to me,
I walked out a little ways.

He had the look of a soul unclaimed,
locked up now but breaking the chains...

When he does...run.
This place cannot handle
the fury of his love...
He will see the world
burn in your name.

# Pinot Noir

Her fingers slipped,  sultry,
the string sliding clean.
The puppet rarely spoke,
but he usually dreamed.
Some nights he awoke
with no love to believe...
A little while later,
he was dancing again...

He danced because he had to,
and the wires were fine.
She thought she moved his body,
but it was really his mind.

The string tied to his chest
sunk deep with a hook.
She'd sell him to the first
peddler to give him a look.

String sunk deep into the base of his soul...
Dancing silly
dancing dirty
dancing for ever more.


One day, the puppet realized
he was damned.
He found the dark lady
with the string in her hand.
"If I was livin', I would quit,
forget how to dance.
I know I'm not a real boy,
but I love like a man. "


The dark lady looked sad,
and it was probably right,
but she strung that puppet long,
and he danced through the night.
Exhausted, he crumbled,
fell down to the floor.
The wire came down around him;
there'd be no dancing no more.

The dark lady felt angry.
A crashed bottle of wishes —
shattered shards at the door,
and the puppet could sense it.
The puppet picked up a jagged piece,
brought it up to his chest.
He slashed himself free
and put the glass to his neck.

He said, "I would've danced forever
If it felt slightly right.
Then glass met wood—
the puppet went into the night.

## V.

SOUGHT ETERNAL,
A DECADE SHADED,
GRIMY MURALS
LEFT FOR THE FUTURE TO DETERMINE.

HE USED TO DREAM LIKE HE WAS CERTAIN.
NOW, HE DOESN'T SLEEP.
MOST OF THE TIME, HE'S HURTING.

INDIAN GIVER.

THE AIR IS BETTER IN HEAVEN.
I WAS THERE FOR A TIME AWHILE BACK...

FOR A MOMENT,
I BLINKED CLOSER...

# Barbeque Blues

The train reeked of white noise, and the moon lurched
orange.
A tinge of pride, laced with power—mixed with powder—
worked and ground and tossed about by the wind.

Sometimes, average people do great things
in a universe far from home
but oh so close—

Perhaps a toast?
A drink to the rustle and the pull
of the things we honor most.

Beyond, they long for me, fleetingly.
It worries me to think that with so much good
raining down from the heavens,
such clarity for falling would arrive.

Clarity is overrated.

There was a time when this man
and this chair worried
whether they needed to or not.

The man is now much better off,
but the chair swims in anxiety.

Fuck you.  I'm trying so very hard.

Something with a "C," basically.
I wonder what sounds so much like leaves. . .

There's a god damned blue rhino
making cheeseburgers in my cerebellum—
should I tell him?

Tell me what?

That at this hour,  there's no time for
dancing dirty on a ballroom drenched with doubt.

That seems reasonable.

# The Vapors

Nothing is really all he ever wanted. Tonight, there was a lot of it. Lucky, lucky. A couple of miles away, a siren broke the peace.

Peaceful enough, though. Sometimes, too much, though.

The teachers used to tell him he'd end up with nothing to show. And nothing was quite a show, indeed!

I suppose if anyone really knew, everyone would be after it. We can't have that.

There's only so much in the night.

Please, go to sleep. Chasing nothing all day long. Laughing when you grasp it. You even feel it. So empty and lonely and right.

There were too many reasons not to say anything.
Fuck, there were even more reasons to say everything.
I said nothing, though.

Honestly? I wondered, the way the night crept long.

Some things never change. Of course, some of those
things are awful. Some of them stalk the night. Still,
I'm not sure how useful the bat would be.

Junkies chasing dragons next to soccer moms steeped ugly
in worry.

Fuck that noise.
When worry wins, you always lose. Sometimes, the
drugs. Other times, the booze. Sometimes, you kick
that shit and wonder how far it'll roll.

Faces in the window tell lies you'll always believe.
Chewing glass, bereaved—wrapped crimson and swaying
with the trees.

A double chocolate vapor of new love, heaved heavy on the breeze.

I am no longer afraid.

# Tributelation

The stains gathered together, most days,
and cheered at the man while he ran errands.
The stains didn't like running, but they **loved** errands.

There was a man named Aaron.

He ran the register most days,
but sometimes he collected carts.
The stains didn't enjoy collecting things,
but some of them called the carts home—
even if they didn't spend all of their time there.

Sometimes, when the man wasn't looking,
and fear was asleep miles away,
the stains wiped themselves all over
his stamp collection.

# Tasteful

As the taste escaped his lips—
the shuddering thud of dancing light crept—
into the waning mind's eye it drifts and drifts...

There were answers cried back
through nostrils and breathed deeply
laughing...
longing...

The chaos called out—
revealed and ingested greedily.
The random beneath the veil...
lucid in its dreamscape—
ever ready and pouring back into him.

None of that jazz.

None wanted, warranted, or required.

Take me back to the beat of fact
on sun splintered dirt.

Drum. Dream.
And question.

# Morgantown

Leaving the craft
on this burning ball of muck.
Don' t touch.
Don' t touch.

One foot for the seamstress
and another for the grave—
don' t delay.
**Don' t** delay. . .

Words at play freshly soldered.
The feet
a little wobble—
stagger,  swim,  now
drowned by it all.

No one.  There is no one.
There is no one!

His heart leapt with joy and
beat back his breath.
He suddenly felt weak,
unprepared for the rest.

No rest to be had, though,
and the fading night's shadow
told tales to a galaxy of one—
that's the fun!

Will you run?

Or take in the solace of the
emptiness as it bends
and winds—
wrapped fresh on the mind.
Never needing to Wonder Walk again.
My friend, this bed's mine.

The eager agony of being the only one—
Gods, the Sun!
It's never shone so solitary and right—

I am the light,
and it is me.
Love, distracted by the plight
and lifted upon the breeze.

This is the beginning of your life again.
No one will ever see it.
That's why it's beautiful.

www.ingramcontent.com/pod-product-compliance
Lightning Source LLC
LaVergne TN
LVHW051758080426
835511LV00018B/3347